W9-BCS-928

Pts 0.5

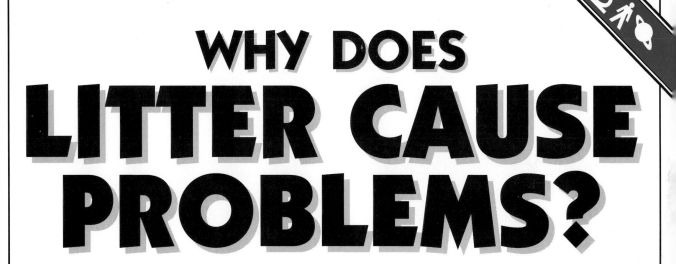

# WHY DOES LITTER CAUSE PROBLEMS?

## BY ISAAC ASIMOV

Gareth Stevens Publishing
**MILWAUKEE**

For a free color catalog describing Gareth Stevens' list of high-quality books, call 1-800-341-3569 (USA) or 1-800-461-9120 (Canada).

Library of Congress Cataloging-in-Publication Data

Asimov, Isaac, 1920-
    Why does litter cause problems? / by Isaac Asimov.
       p.  cm. -- (Ask Isaac Asimov)
    Includes bibliographical references and index.
    Summary: Discusses how litter damages our environment
and how to dispose of it properly.
    ISBN 0-8368-0799-5
   1. Litter (Trash)--Environmental aspects--Juvenile literature.
2. Refuse and refuse disposal--Environmental aspects--Juvenile
literature. [1. Litter (Trash) 2. Refuse and refuse disposal.
3. Pollution] I. Title. II. Series: Asimov, Isaac, 1920-  Ask
Isaac Asimov.
TD813.A84   1992
363.72--dc20                  92-5349

Edited, designed, and produced by
**Gareth Stevens Publishing**
1555 North RiverCenter Drive, Suite 201
Milwaukee, Wisconsin 53212, USA

Text © 1992 by Nightfall, Inc., and Martin H. Greenberg
End matter © 1992 by Gareth Stevens, Inc.
Format © 1992 by Gareth Stevens, Inc.

**Picture Credits**
pp. 2-3, Rick Karpinski, 1992; pp. 4-5, © G. D. Plage/Bruce Coleman Limited; pp. 6-7, © Dick Scott-Stewart/ IMPACT Photos; pp. 8-9, Rick Karpinski, 1992; p. 9 (inset), © Tom McCarthy/Third Coast Stock Source; pp. 10-11, © H. Armstrong Roberts; pp. 12-13, © Doug Sokell/Visuals Unlimited; pp. 14-15, © Kim Taylor/Bruce Coleman Limited; pp. 16-17, © David Woodfall/NHPA; p. 16 (inset), © John Cancalosi/Bruce Coleman Limited; pp. 18-19, © David Woodfall/NHPA; pp. 20-21, © Daniel Dancer/Still Pictures; pp. 22-23, © Julie Fryer/Bruce Coleman Limited; p. 24, © Julie Fryer/Bruce Coleman Limited

Cover photograph, © Jane Burton/Bruce Coleman Limited: Brown rats pause on a garbage dump. Litter attracts rats that can spread disease and that sometimes attack humans and other animals.

Series editor: Elizabeth Kaplan
Editor: Valerie Weber
Series designer: Sabine Beaupré
Picture researcher: Diane Laska

Printed in MEXICO

1 2 3 4 5 6 7 8 9 98 97 96 95 94 93 92

# Contents

Words printed in **boldface** type the first time they occur in the text appear in the glossary.

## Exploring Our Environment

Look around you. You see forests, fields, lakes, and rivers. You see farms, factories, houses, and cities. All of these things make up our **environment**. Sometimes there are problems with the environment. For example, **litter** lines city streets, floats down rivers, washes up on beaches, and blows through parks. There's even litter in space. Why does litter cause problems? Let's find out.

5

## Use It Once, Toss It Out

We live in a **disposable** world.  So many
things are made to be used only once and
then thrown away.  Paper cups, plastic
silverware, cans, and soft drink bottles
are thrown out by the ton every day.  But
sometimes people do not get rid of these and
other items properly.  Instead of throwing
them in garbage cans or **recycling** bins, they
toss them out a car window or drop them
on the ground.  Any item disposed of
improperly is called litter.

7

## Littering Made Easy

Many things we buy come **overpackaged**.
Think of your favorite fast-food lunch. Each
item comes in its own separate container.
Some foods are even double wrapped to keep
them warm. They all get put in a bag which,
along with your drink, is stuck in a disposable
tray. Even your straw comes individually
wrapped. You sit down at a picnic table to eat
your lunch. As you unwrap your food, paper
starts blowing in the wind. No wonder we
have so much litter!

## An Ugly Mess and a Horrible Waste

Litter causes lots of problems. For one thing, litter is ugly. We don't like to look at rusted cans along the roadside. We get annoyed when sheets of dirty newspaper blow up against our homes.

Local governments have to hire workers to pick up litter. This costs a lot of money. If people didn't litter, the money could be spent on other things.

11

## Ruining the Beautiful

Litter can destroy nature. For example, a cigarette butt carelessly tossed on a layer of dry pine needles can start a fire that will burn down an entire forest.

Litter can also turn nature's most beautiful places into **eyesores**. Imagine having to kick a path through aluminum cans to get a view of a rushing waterfall. When you reach the pool below the waterfall, you notice it is junked up with floating garbage. You are more aware of the litter than of the waterfall.

## Germs, Germs, Germs

Litter helps spread **disease**. **Germs** that cause disease multiply on litter. Litter also attracts insects and animals that spread germs. For example, germs grow on bits of food stuck to a discarded hamburger wrapper. If a fly lands on the food wrapper, it picks up germs on its feet. If the fly later lands on a counter where food is prepared, the germs can spread. Someone eating the food prepared at that counter might get sick.

14

## Tides of Litter

Litter tossed out at sea washes up on beaches thousands of miles away. Plastic bags, torn fishing nets, bottle caps, and broken toys all come in with the tides.

But spoiling beaches is only one problem caused by tides of litter. Some animals that live in the oceans accidentally eat scraps of litter. Then the animals get very sick. Other animals get tangled in floating plastic nets or get plastic rings from six packs of cans caught around their neck. Many choke and die.

## Fighting Litter Everywhere

Countries have laws against littering. People who dump garbage along a road can be fined. Some places have laws requiring that glass, aluminum, tin cans, plastics, and paper be recycled. People are less likely to litter if they know they can get money for their garbage.

Some companies are making plastics that are **biodegradable**. These plastics break down when they are exposed to sunlight or to certain chemicals.

18

## How Can You Help?

The best way to help solve the litter problem
is not to litter yourself. Throw all garbage
in garbage cans and put **recyclables** — like
the ones arranged here in the recycling
symbol — in recycling bins. Instead of buying
disposable or overpackaged products, buy
products that are reusable. Figure out new
things to do with bags, packages, and other
used things. Ask your friends and family to
do the same. To fight litter all over the world,
join groups of people who pick up litter in
public places. You can also support
organizations working to prevent litter at sea.

21

# The World's Better Off Without Litter

Littering isn't a new problem. For thousands of years, people have gotten rid of things they didn't want by dropping them on the ground or in the sea. But with our planet so crowded with people, we can no longer afford to be sloppy with our trash. By cleaning up litter and by reducing the amount of litter we produce, we can help make our world a better place for everyone.

# More Books to Read

*Avoid Littering* by Roger J. Himmel (Society for Visual Education)
*Garbage: Our Endangered Planet* by Karen O'Connor (Lucent Books)
*Space Garbage* by Isaac Asimov (Gareth Stevens)

# Places to Write

Here are some places you can write to for more information about garbage and littering. Be sure to tell them exactly what you want to know about. Give them your full name and address so they can write back to you.

Institute of Scrap Recycling
   Industries, Inc.
P.O. Box 27718
Washington, D.C. 20038-7718

Greenpeace Foundation
185 Spadina Avenue, 6th Floor
Toronto, Ontario M5T 2C6

National Marine Fisheries Service
Office of Protected Resources
Marine Debris Program
1335 East-West Highway
Silver Spring, Maryland 20910

# Glossary

**disease** (dih-ZEEZ): an unhealthy condition of the body; illness.

**disposable** (dihs-POZE-uh-buhl): meant to be used briefly and then thrown away.

**environment** (en-VIE-run-ment): the natural and artificial things that make up the Earth.

**eyesore**: something that is ugly to look at.

**germ** (jurm): a tiny living cell that can cause disease.

23

**litter** (LIHT-ter): anything that is disposed of improperly.

**overpackaged** (oh-ver-PACK-uhjd): a product comes with more wrapping than necessary; many fast foods, cosmetics, and supermarket items are overpackaged.

**recyclables** (ree-SIE-kluh-bulz): items that can be recycled.

**recycle** (ree-SIE-kuhl): to melt down or shred a material and process it so that it can be made into the same or similar material again.

## Index

*15005*